We Hope This Reaches You in Time

We Hope This Reaches You in Time

Samantha King Holmes and r.h. Sin

Andrews McMeel
PUBLISHING®

contents

Samantha King Holmes

r.h. Sin

section one

by

Samantha King Holmes

I'm never really quite sure with you
You've walked out on me multiple times
Now, I wait
Not for you to realize the damage you've done
Just for you to come back
To come down from the hate and resentment
you have stored in your soul for me
Why would you want to keep that? Keep me?
We talked about kids earlier tonight
I told you I wanted two, maybe three
Do you ever face yourself, the version of you
that strangles all of the good out of me?

Samantha King Holmes

Knees hugging my chest
Tears streaming down my temples
Hands crushing into the waves of emotions
leaking from my eyes, as if that's going to stop it
The worst feeling in the world is to suffer in pain
and have no one to talk to
To truly be alone while your thoughts wander
away with you into this abyss of self-pity and
torment
"You aren't different. Told you that you'd be
right back here. They never really cared about
you,"
An inner monologue conveying its discontent
Some statements false, others true
Things that have come to light
Others that I'm subconsciously aware of but
don't want to admit
Trapped in a prison of overthinking
There's a part of me that wants to fight, and the
other part just wants a reprieve
I've given so much already

You ever watch your joy slip through your fingers,
but no matter how much you clasp your hands
together to save it, it keeps going?
That's what it felt like to love you in the end
My hands are still aching

Samantha King Holmes

4

I want to write you the fairy tale
that life hasn't given you
Administer that peace of mind
Help you forgive yourself for all the times
you cried from believing in lies
Perilously giving yourself to another
If no one has told you
You should love yourself more

I can't stand the sound of my heart breaking again
So, I sing louder, dance harder, write with such a
raw intensity
Anything to drown out the destruction
I just want to feel something besides constant
disappointment

Samantha King Holmes

I crawled up beside you
You draped your arm over me and rubbed me
until I fell asleep
Some people desire fame, some riches
I desire nothing more than a lifetime of
being cradled safely under your arm, freely
dreaming

I don't know how to fix this
Pinpoint where it all started to go bad
The fights continue way into the night
until every jab is thrown
We depart from exhaustion
In the moment, we regret little of what was said
Drip by drip, it seeps in
The realization that this has gotten much worse
than foreseen
Does "I'm sorry" still work, or have we run that
into the ground?
The prospect of not being right for one another
looming
There's no measurement for how much that hurts

Samantha King Holmes

The floor is worn from my pacing
Soul restlessly distraught from my obsessing
Love, I want no more of you
I resent what I've allowed you to do to me
I willingly gave my all
Only to be left with the remnants of me
Devoured, you consumed me completely

Give me refuge from my craze
Let there be understanding where there was once
anger
Let me be disciplined where I used to be
impulsive
Let me be strong when I want to cave in and cry
Help me to forgive but retain the wisdom that
pain has taught me
Give me solace when my mind knows no rest
Stop the self-indulgent need to seek vengeance
What I have allowed to diminish me thus far
doesn't deserve the power
I want to love life like I once did

Samantha King Holmes

None of us enjoys watching someone whom we care about be hurt. We go out of our way to make them smile, even if it's just a little. We listen as they analyze a situation repeatedly, wondering what could have been done differently. We give advice, we see things differently, and in the end, we just want to make things better. The truth is it isn't always that simple. Sometimes we have to let people work things out on their own. It's better overall when someone has come to a resolution themselves versus feeling they were pushed into a specific direction. Sometimes people need to know that they aren't alone and that they can lean on someone when needed.

When you finally start talking to the universe,
you may be surprised what the response will be.
Listen closely.

Samantha King Holmes

Figure out what it is that you want out of life and move in that direction.

People think I don't give a fuck about anyone.
They're wrong; that's not the issue.
I care about way too many people who don't
give a fuck about me.

Samantha King Holmes

If you let people tell you who you are
for too long, they'll look at you with
disgust when you correct them.

Be mindful of those who don't support you, but decide to support those who stand against you.

I will minimize your place in my life till your absence is no longer an issue.

We've all been there. Feeling around in the dark
for some kind of meaning. Feeling less and
less like ourselves, depleted, drained. Always
searching for something, a reason to be rooted
to. I think we go through so much that we don't
stop and process. We endure, but we don't
stop and give ourselves time to take in what
happened. We move on, push forward, until the
next thing comes along and forces us to once
again have something to work through. Stop for
a second and let it all sink in. Appreciate where
you are, how far you've come, and give yourself
credit for what you made it out of. Just give
yourself a moment to sit with things. Don't run
from them.

Samantha King Holmes

You can't force someone to have the same vision as you. You can't force them to be on the same page. I think the goal is to find someone who understands that a relationship takes work and that it won't always be perfect, but it is more than worth staying in and working on.

Some people just take from your life. You give repeatedly, as if you have to prove something to them, and then one day, you stop. You realize that even though you may have their best interest in mind, you can't say the same for them. It's ok to no longer entertain people who don't make you feel good when you're around them.

Samantha King Holmes

We hold on to the potential of someone so strongly that we completely disregard whether they see that within themselves. We tell ourselves they will be better, that we will make them better, but never question why we have to or why we obligate ourselves to the task while disregarding the neglect we ourselves endure. Don't stress yourself out over trying to make someone else better while you're suffering.

Sometimes we stay with people because we tell ourselves that they're the best life has to offer us. It's a reflection of how we feel about ourselves and what we think we deserve. There are other times when we let people break us down and manipulate us into thinking that no one else will love us or care. The best thing you can do for yourself is to not only know but also to love who you are so someone else can't come along and define your value.

Samantha King Holmes

Don't make excuses for someone not reciprocating what you give. You deserve someone who's supportive and brings you happiness. Filter out people who don't have a positive impact on your life.

The misconception that nothing has changed. I think that's the maddening part for us to wrap our minds around. The one thing we don't want to admit to ourselves. How did it get here? When? Why? All valid questions. What's next? I think that's the scary part. It's having to come to terms with the fact that what we had in our mind of what this could have been and what the reality is are two different things. Don't cling to someone all for the sake of having someone. You deserve happiness too.

We willingly bleed ourselves dry for those we care about without ever stopping to question, when is it enough?

We're hard on ourselves when things don't work out. It's not enough that it didn't go the way we thought; we have to punish ourselves for it. It's our fault that we weren't what someone wanted or needed. There has to be something wrong with us. We're lacking in some way. I think we need to stop putting ourselves down every time someone can't see something within us. Ok, things ended, it hurts, I get that. Chalking it all up to you somehow being "lesser than" or anything of the sort is detrimental. You're not going to be compatible with every single person you find yourself interested in; that's ok. You just need to realize that it is ok and learn what you will from the experience without tearing yourself down in the process.

Samantha King Holmes

People are constantly trying to soften the blow, anticipating that the person they are with is going to hurt them. If you can't trust that the person you're with isn't going to cause you some form of pain, why are you even with them? It's like people are just holding on to someone, anyone, while trying to find something better.

That's not the way you should go about it. At some point, you're going to have to give a relationship a fair shot. It should also be a rule of thumb that if you feel something is off or you can't completely trust someone, there is no real need to move forward. Trust, communication, and loyalty are essential for a healthy relationship.

You're going to fall for people who may not be able to reciprocate what you give. People who won't love you the way you love them. They may not even allow themselves to get so deep into the emotion that it's even genuine when they say those three words. The truth is not everyone you love is going to be for you. It happens. That doesn't mean you won't eventually find someone who is.

Samantha King Holmes

Cause there will be days where it's hard, even seems impossible. No matter the pressure or doubt, keep moving forward.

Do more than just survive your relationships.

Samantha King Holmes

You can't force someone to respect you. You can't force them to be loyal or kind. You can't force someone to be patient. Ultimately, you can't force someone to be someone they're not. What you can do, though, is acknowledge who someone really is and evaluate whether a relationship is worth the effort. Sacrificing yourself, your happiness, your peace, your needs and wants doesn't save a relationship. Also, you shouldn't have to sacrifice all that just to have one.

There are bruises you can't see. Wounds you won't ever know about. Things that have eaten away at my soul all because I'm the kind of person who's loved all the wrong kinds of people too hard. I've moved forward, I've grown from it, but that doesn't mean there aren't scars. Looking at them now just isn't as painful.

Samantha King Holmes

Sometimes letting go isn't the loss you think it is. Sometimes it's easy and for a good reason. Sometimes when you put yourself first, you realize that people aren't as great as you made them out to be in your head. That's ok. Progress and growth don't always have to be seen as a hardship.

Don't let feeling lonely be a gateway to letting people who aren't really for you into your life.

Samantha King Holmes

We forget to stop and process. Give ourselves a second to debrief what occurred. Most times we just want to get over the part where it hurts. We go through it but forget to take whatever lesson we could have from it with us. Stop running. The pain is going to be there; it doesn't go away instantly. It will over time. You can leave with something from it, though, that may help you later; your choice.

A flaw of being a giver is that sometimes you're so busy giving to others that you forget to replenish yourself. So eventually you're drained and you realize that no one you were giving to filled you with anything.

Samantha King Holmes

Be mindful of the version someone sells you versus who they actually are.

You have more going for yourself than what
once was. I think sometimes in our mourning
of what's been lost we forget to look around and
remember what we do have. I don't understand
why we reach out and hold on so tightly to the
things that didn't work out. I guess it's possibly
the finality of it all and what we choose to
see as unanswered questions, or maybe we
can't understand how we were so wrong about
something. Either way, at some point you have
to come up for air and realize you have so much
to smile about if you stop focusing on what
didn't go the way you anticipated.

Samantha King Holmes

The people of this world can be so draining.

I don't think anything quite shakes us to the core like change. We like comfort; we stay where we've been cause it's all we know. Thing is, that's not always good for us. You're not meant to stay dormant or complacent in a space that renders you no peace. No one likes being uncomfortable, I get it, but how is being in pain a better option? It's ok to make a shift if it suits your best interest. Stop questioning whether you deserve happiness or feeling fulfilled; that's not something you need to question.

Samantha King Holmes

At some point the excuses have to end. Aren't you tired of feeling drained and disrespected by the person who's supposed to have your back?

Don't let these people use you up for their own pleasure. You deserve to be nurtured and adored. Stop settling for one-word responses and delayed interactions from someone not mature enough to even handle an actual relationship.

Samantha King Holmes

There are times when you know you should let go, but for some reason or another you linger a bit. It's this hope that somehow there's still a chance for things to get better even when there's not.

Sometimes the best thing you can do for yourself is to see something as it is rather than trying to make it seem better.

Samantha King Holmes

That's what gets us, the fantasy. This thing we keep replaying over and over in our head. A lifeline that keeps what we know isn't working going. The belief that one day this person is going to wake up and magically get it. They will appreciate us, treat us better, love us, and we finally get to have that happily ever after we keep hearing about. How long do you think before they will start to see how wonderful you are and actually treat you the way you deserve? Better question, how long are you willing to wait and see? Tough question, why do you think so little of yourself and so much more of this person that you feel you need to wait for them to see how good of a person you are to be happy? Heavy stuff, right? Yeah, I know. Sleep on it. At some point, though, you may want to face the tough questions.

There are just some wounds
that apologies don't heal.

Samantha King Holmes

There are people who will say they're your friends, say they'll be there if you ever need them, but conveniently disappear when you're in a pinch or just feeling low. What I've learned is that some people just like being around when things are "fun, light," but when things get serious, they can't handle it. They don't know how to. Instead of just being honest and saying that, they wait for you to figure things out on your own and then come back after the dust has settled. Life isn't always going to be easy; it just won't be. You need and deserve people who know that and won't abandon you when you need someone to lean on.

Don't look for others to "fix" you. They can't
see all your wounds; they don't know your pain
like you. You have to put that time into yourself
to heal, but don't expect others to do it for you.

Samantha King Holmes

You're still here and you're working through it. There is nothing wrong with that. Give yourself a break.

We question why people come back, make it seem like fate, romanticize it. We don't stop and ask why we let them back in so easily. Like maybe our hesitance, utter refusal to let go and let be, is the exact reason why we don't move forward and they keep rolling back in.

Samantha King Holmes

We say we love ourselves but allow others to mistreat us. How?

We cling to others because we feel like we won't be able to do better. If you keep telling yourself that, then that's all you'll ever believe.

Samantha King Holmes

People treat self-love like it's a destination, like after they reach this certain point, everything will be better and fall into place. It's a process. There are going to be days when you doubt yourself, when you feel everything is just going wrong. There are going to be moments when you wish things were different, that you were different. That's stuff that you work through. It happens. You don't have to be or feel perfect every single day. It's about being kind to yourself and forgiving when you aren't. Self-love is loving yourself in all conditions.

Don't let anyone take advantage of your vulnerability. Not everyone who's there in your hour of need has good intentions.

Samantha King Holmes

It's important to know what you need out of a relationship and what you will or won't tolerate. Don't feel pressured to adjust your standards just to find someone.

We are resilient, we are passionate, and we are strong, even though most days we may not think that. We will stand and push forward even when we feel broken. We will give our all to hold something up even without help. We will stay and mourn the demise of something we thought was great, because we believed in the potential.

It's ok to walk away. It's ok to do what's best for you. Starting over is hard, but staying in something that has already come to an end won't do much for you. You deserve someone who will put in as much effort as you, if not more. It's ok to save yourself. You don't need to wait for someone to come along and do it for you.

Samantha King Holmes

Some lessons are painful. The mistake that's made far too often is failing to learn from them.

You know that feeling. That moment when you look up and no longer recognize the person in front of you. You stop and question when the change happened. When they stopped being familiar. You hold on cause you're hoping that person comes back; and when they don't, you mourn. You mourn time, the effort, and ultimately this dream in your head where you had it all figured out. It happens. Don't let it defeat you.

Samantha King Holmes

Healing isn't easy. There are going to be days when it hurts, when it feels like you're not going to get through it. You will.

I don't think we take time for ourselves to just have a break and reflect on what happened. I think sometimes we just move on to the next thing that comes along and carry our unresolved feelings into that. I think we need to change this narrative that tells us that the best way to forget a person is to move on to the next one. People go from relationship to relationship without realizing they're pretty much dating the same kind of person over and over again. How much time and effort would have been saved if they just stopped for a second to reflect on that? We have to do better for ourselves. We need to change the strategy we've been using.

Samantha King Holmes

Be mindful of whom you decide
to plant your roots within.

Just like love, I don't think the word "friend" should be used lightly. There is so much substance to it. A lot of people don't have as many friends as they would like to believe, but a lot of acquaintances. That's fine. A small group of people, or even a person, whom you can truly rely on is way better than having a squad of people whom you really aren't sure about.

Samantha King Holmes

The truth is some people just aren't as good as we make them out to be. I'm not saying people don't change. Just that ignoring their behavior isn't going to assist with that.

We've become so good, too good, at wearing masks. At saying we're ok when we don't mean it and suffering alone because we don't reach out and ask for help. You don't have to pretend to be "ok" on your own.

Samantha King Holmes

I think at times we tend to rush into things. We don't always think things through or listen to our gut when those little red flags pop up. Don't try to convince yourself that something is better than what it is. One way or another, the truth shows itself. Don't let yourself become collateral damage in the process.

section two

by

r.h. Sin

You're moving on, you're letting go, but you
still miss him because you genuinely cared.

r.h. Sin

I want to speak directly to you because you've been so hard on yourself this year. I know you entered this year with many hopes and dreams. You wanted something different, you were tired of heartache. Tired of pain, weary from fighting for someone who refused to fight for you.

Here you are now, on this day, this night, still suffering. Wondering to yourself, "When will it get better?" You may not realize this, but despite your brokenness, you are stronger than you've been. Despite the chaotic feelings that live within you, there is still a lot of love and strength left within your heart and soul.

It can be difficult moving on, letting go. None of that is easy for the person who cares genuinely for those they love, and that is no different for you. Your heart is unlike anything most people have ever known, and your love is full, even when you feel empty. You are enough even when others make you feel like you aren't, and you will continue to be more than enough despite feeling broken.

I know we don't know each other, but I'd like
to think that you are reading this for a reason.
It's 6:09 in the morning where I am, and I'm
not sure when or where this will reach you, but
hopefully it does and hopefully it helps. I know
I'm just a stranger, but I care, especially after
you've taken the time to read this. I'll continue
to share things like this, just as long as you
promise to never give up on yourself.

Thank you for being so damn strong!

r.h. Sin

I don't think you should try harder for someone who rarely tries for you. I don't think you should spend time on someone who can't make time for you, and I don't think you should feel guilty about walking away from a person who has proven to be someone you can never depend on.

Somewhere right now, someone is tired of wasting their time, energy, and love. Maybe that someone is reading this currently. I know it's hard to believe in real love when all you've known is heartache, but I think it's time to choose yourself, to love yourself. I think it's time for you to walk toward the exit, leave behind anyone who keeps your heart from smiling. It's difficult because you care so much, but it's time to redirect that energy and focus it on yourself. This year will be over before you know it, and I hope you do whatever it is you need to do to find your peace of mind. I believe in you. I won't give up on you . . . no matter how happy I become in my own life. I will not leave you behind.

r.h. Sin

Because that's the thing about falling in love with the wrong person: it doesn't always happen quickly. It takes time, and it'll also take time to move forward without that person.

The realization that arguing with someone who prefers to disappoint you is a complete waste of energy and time. Energy that is best invested in yourself and time that should only be given to things that make you happy.

r.h. Sin

When men get upset about the subject matter of my content and the fact that I'm uplifting women, I think they fail to realize that any content that puts no-good men on notice is also content that is supportive of good men. Now, if you're triggered by something I've said, maybe you fit the character of the type of man I'm telling these women to avoid.

Most men will never be strong enough to choose you. And that's not your issue. You never lose when a weak man loses his position in your life.

r.h. Sin

Opinions can't harm you when you know yourself.

Some people will fail you, even when you've given them your all. It's easy to blame yourself when, in all honesty, the truth is . . . not everyone has the heart you have, and it's okay to walk away from those who do not appreciate the energy you give them.

r.h. Sin

Notes on Letting Go

You've done all you can. You've given second chances. You stayed longer than you should have, and now you're ready to face the realization that maybe it's time to let go.

Your heart is weary, and so is your mind as you've been overwhelmed with the fear of starting over. You often give up on letting go because you're afraid of being alone, and yet, whenever you're with them, you feel like you're the only one trying, and that itself is the loneliest feeling.

Moving on doesn't happen overnight. There are moments where you will miss that person even after you've walked away. That's just part of the process. That's only part of the event of letting go. Take your time and feel whatever it is you need to feel while you are embarking on the journey of setting yourself free.

Letting go will probably be one of the hardest things you've ever done because, deep down, you truly did love this person. But what is love to someone who will never appreciate and/or honor your heart and your devotion? Trying harder for someone who never tries for you will never make them the one. Loving the wrong person will never make them the one. And you're reading this now because you realize that it may be time for you to choose yourself finally, and I HOPE THIS HELPS.

r.h. Sin

You undersell yourself whenever you settle for a relationship that will never match your ideas of love.

What is meant for you will come, even through storms.

r.h. Sin

Be a rose with thorns. Soft but tough.

grab a sword
guard your heart

r.h. Sin

Strangers will have the most to say about you,
and what they think of you will always be based
on how much they hate themselves for being
incapable of achieving what you've accomplished.

you can either run from the storm
or become more like rain

if you love someone
who hurts you
set them free

she, like the caterpillar,
found a way to make the end
a new beginning

r.h. Sin

Pain and heartache are just another opportunity to become stronger.

Your presence is a gift. Be mindful of who you share it with.

r.h. Sin

she found refuge within herself
she found love within the walls
of her own heart

in peace, love heals
in war, love hurts

the battle has begun
he's no longer on your side

r.h. Sin

kind soul, big heart
you are a lost art
and I hope you find yourself

We Hope This Reaches You in Time

a woman who settles
is an angel
who has forgotten
her ability to fly

r.h. Sin

You're a good woman who seems to have rewarded yourself with a relationship that sours your heart. You've placed your kind heart in the hands of someone who will only make you cold, and I hope you find the courage to set that bridge on fire because they no longer deserve a path to reach you. I hope you set that bridge on fire and keep yourself warm with the flames.

Lies are a weak man's truth, and whenever he speaks, he's telling you who he truly is. Listen, then ignore and avoid him.

r.h. Sin

There is nothing wilder than finding a love that feels free. A love that feels pure. A love that doesn't cause you to compromise your peace of mind and emotional health. A love that doesn't require you to feel lost and neglected. A love that only demands that you grow strong enough to conquer the pains that come from existing in a chaotic world.

Holding on to the wrong person is like expecting the desert to grow roses.

r.h. Sin

Honor yourself by detaching your heart from
those who betray it.

Be fearless and leave him behind.

I have way too much respect for myself to allow
anyone the opportunity to treat me like shit.
Over the years, I've learned that even family
can be a version of the enemy, and sometimes
they're best placed in the past. It may be
difficult, but anyone who hurts your heart should
be removed from your life immediately.

Stop holding a candle for a lover who would
rather you live in darkness.

r.h. Sin

You fit perfectly in my regrets.

Along the way, I learned that you were no longer worthy of being missed, and even though we ended, you were never a loss, and I was always worth it.

r.h. Sin

Your ex is just a story that is no longer worth being told.

You shouldn't have to convince him that you are worth being respected. That's not how love works.

Everyone talks about what they want their love to look like instead of what they want that love to feel like, and this is why my generation can feel so lonely, even in the presence of the person they claim to love.

Know the game. Not so you can play it but so you can avoid being played.

The cracks in your heart are reminders that you have always been brave enough to love even when others lacked the courage to love you back, and there is nothing wrong with that.

Cheating is not something to understand. It's a reason to end all means of contact.

r.h. Sin

Suffering strengthened the wall in front of my heart.

Some friends just love you in a way that family can't.

r.h. Sin

Don't let him use your fear of loneliness against you.

You are the flower, your family the roots, and
sometimes you're forced to grow from tainted
seeds. And no matter how damaged your
upbringing may have been, you survive, and you
flourish despite it all.

r.h. Sin

I wish I waited longer to be an adult. I wanted so badly to be grown that I buried my childhood as soon as I got my hands on a shovel.

When you're restless, you feel mentally attacked by every memory you've struggled to forget, and every person who no longer deserves to be on your mind finds a way to keep you up at night.

r.h. Sin

If he missed you, he'd find a way to be by your
side, and if he loves you, then why are you
always so sad? . . .

Instead of telling her how you feel, you
allow her mind to drag itself through a pit of
uncertainty. You play this game of push and pull.
You're hot then cold as this cycle continues.
You are leaving her to question not only you but
herself for staying as long as she has. You break
her down then build her up with empty promises
and no intent to truly change your ways. This
hurts. The way you mistreat her when she's done
nothing but love you, all of this hurts.

r.h. Sin

Liars are weak. Lying is a confession of weakness. Sadly, many relationships are plagued with lies, and those lies are the very thing that has brought you here to this book and to this page. You deserve someone who is strong enough to be transparent. You deserve someone who doesn't manipulate you with empty promises. Understand that people will say anything just to get what they want out of you, and though it may be difficult to tell whether a person is telling you the truth . . . it's important to pay attention to that gut feeling, that natural intuition you have. Deep down, you know the truth, even when you choose to ignore it. For whatever reason, you may have decided to overlook their inconsistencies and lies, but you mustn't continue to settle for someone who isn't living up to your idea of what it means to be in a healthy relationship. No more allowing your heart to be lied to. No more allowing your heart to remain in hands too weak to hold it.

Disloyalty is the destruction of peace. A partner who is unfaithful destroys the very foundation of a relationship. So many of you know what it means to be with someone who turns out to be disloyal, and you also know the struggles of letting go of that person. It's important to always be loyal to yourself. And what I mean by that is . . . if someone is unfaithful to you, if the person you're with betrays you . . . then you must choose yourself. It may be difficult, but you owe it to yourself to want more for yourself, and the only way to find someone as loyal as you is to always walk away from those who betray you.

r.h. Sin

Single women are not always lonely or empty. There are a lot of single women who are filled with peace and joy because they are more than enough for themselves.

You will be someone's best thing, but until then, be the best for yourself.

r.h. Sin

You tried, you fought. You made an effort, you
offered forgiveness. You've given second and
third chances, but nothing changes. It bothers me
to know that you know you've done all that you
can and yet you continue to blame yourself.
Stop.
Stop.
Fuck that.
STOP.
You can't force love in a relationship that isn't
worthy of your energy. It's not your job to keep
a man. It's time to choose yourself. Okay?

Strangely enough, he has trust issues but expects you to trust him. He says he doesn't want to be in a relationship, and yet he expects you to treat him like your boyfriend. This type of man is weak and unworthy of your energy and attention.

r.h. Sin

Settling is the enemy of true love.

Men who are confused about the way they feel
about you are the enemy of peace and happiness.
Avoid them.

r.h. Sin

I hope you learn to detach from anyone who is
no longer worthy of your devotion and love. I
hope you find the strength to break away from
anyone who attempts to break you down.

It's not your fault, and you are not obligated
to tolerate this mistreatment. I can say that as
a man and from my own personal experience.
I could appreciate and acknowledge the love
that my wife has given me only because I love
myself. Men who hate themselves tend to take
it out on their partner. You don't have to stay
where you feel unappreciated, nor do you need
to blame yourself for his inability to love you.
Again, it's not your fault.

Relationships should promote happiness, peace,
and emotional growth. Anything less than that
is not a relationship; it's hell. Free yourself, take
care.

r.h. Sin

Dear reader,

I don't know you, but it hurts me to know that you're not happy. And I just want to apologize on behalf of my gender and all the times that men who were unworthy of you decided to break your heart. You deserve so much more than what he's willing to give, and I just hope you find the strength to set yourself free.

Sincerely,
r.h. Sin

People are always talking about how hard marriage is. They rarely tell you how easy it is when you marry the right person.

r.h. Sin

You are more than enough.
You are fully capable of letting him go.
You have done all you can.
You have reached your breaking point.
You're not happy with him, and you're realizing this more and more as you read these words.
You're broken, you're tired, but you are powerful enough to break free.
You're afraid of starting over. Sometimes you feel stuck. Most times you plan over and over in your head how you'll leave, but then you often believe that moving on may be impossible.
You're reading this now, and maybe it helps, maybe it doesn't. Maybe you'll save these words, maybe you'll just ignore me and close this book.
You're afraid, but you're brave and mighty.
Don't give up on yourself. I won't give up on you.

She is you, all powerful and capable of evolving even when others wish to prevent you from building up the courage to grow and let go. This year has been tough, and yet here you are, still standing, at times not knowing how much further you'll be able to go, but you're here reading these words. I don't think it's too late. Sure, you've spent some time in a relationship that drains your spirit. You've spent many moments struggling with letting go because your feelings were always honest, you just fell for a liar who has always been good at saying the right things while proving to be incapable of making good on their promises. They say "Sorry," then continue to do the things they apologize for. They claim to love you even while they act as if they hate you.

You've come here in search of something that'll keep you going. You've come here in search of some version of hope, a reminder that things will get better. Something written to help you feel stronger. I can't pretend to know exactly how you're feeling while reading this, but I will say this to you . . . you'd have to be one hell of a mighty woman to still be standing after all you've been through, and I'm just the stranger who cares. This is not about me. This was written for and inspired by whoever needs it. I believe these words will reach the right person. If you happen to come upon these words in your moment of need, then I've accomplished something, and if for some reason this doesn't reach you, I'll keep trying.

r.h. Sin

You're restless because you've fallen for someone who is nothing like they promised. You feel hopeless, and yet you're holding on to that person because of the time you've invested in trying to make it work. Your heart is breaking because you've come to the realization that no amount of effort will make them right for you.

Nights like this are the most difficult for you, and this is why you're here. This is why you're holding this book, reading these words in search of an answer, and while I have you here. I just want you to know that you will always be more than enough. I want you to know that you are truly capable of moving on. I want you to know that, despite the heartache you've suffered, you deserve to be fought for, you deserve to be cherished, you deserve to be loved. And for those of you who will thank me for this message, understand that it's all you. Give yourself the credit. You deserve it. You're a survivor, and I'm proud of you.

They never think you're hurting because you're brave and strong. You've hidden so much pain behind a smile. You smother your screams with laughter, but I just want you to know that you are not alone and you are not invisible.

r.h. Sin

Moving on because you deserve more. Moving on because you love yourself. Moving on because you deserve the truth, a transparency that feels good to the soul. Moving on because you can, because you're capable. Moving on because you are strong enough to break free from a relationship that isn't worth your energy. Moving on because you're tired of feeling alone, tired of being neglected. Tired of suffering, fighting to survive the pain of being with the wrong person. Moving on because there is joy in leaving behind anyone who no longer fits into your idea of happiness. Moving on because you relate to everything on this page.

It's been a long time coming. You've done all you can. You've given your all in trying to attempt to save a relationship that is no longer worthy of your attention. You don't have to hate that person, but you do have to love yourself enough to walk away.

r.h. Sin

Today, this afternoon, and tonight. Make sure you do more of what makes you happy, and stay away from cowards who will never be capable of appreciating you.

You're always fighting for him, but who fights for you? Always giving your all, but who tries for you? I know you might love him, but that in no way is an excuse to allow your heart to sit in hands unworthy of your love. I know you're afraid of being alone, but you already feel alone whenever you're with him. I know it's hard, it's difficult to let go, but aren't you always doing the impossible, aren't you always surviving things meant to destroy you? While you're conflicted about giving up on him, it's important to know that staying with him means giving up on yourself. It's time to choose yourself; it's time to love yourself more than he ever will. Let him go, because holding on to him means losing yourself. Let him go, and you'll find the love and joy you need, and you'll find that love and joy within your own heart because you are more than capable of giving yourself everything he refuses to give you. I'm not sure if my words matter, I'm not sure if these words will reach you, but if these words do matter, and if you're reading this now . . . I hope you know I'll never give up on reminding you that you are deserving of so much more than what you've had. I need you to read this, believe this, and use this to your benefit and come back to these words whenever you feel like you're stuck. Take care.

r.h. Sin

You can't find love until you've detached from the person who treats you as if they hate you. You can't find peace until you've decided to walk away from the person who has caused so much chaos within your heart, and you will not find joy until you choose to search from within. You can do all things on your own. Your love is more than enough to replenish your soul, and the joy you've searched for in others has always lived within you.

It's easy to think that a relationship with someone will solve all of your problems, and while having a significant other can be beautiful, it's important to also focus on the relationship you have with yourself. Maybe after all the pain you've experienced in relationships with others, it's time to focus on yourself for a bit. After all the fight and energy and time you've given to someone who was never worthy, maybe it's time to fight for yourself and everything you believe you deserve out of this life.

Sometimes you have to do a family and friends detox.

r.h. Sin

he left you in the middle of the sea
then returned with his hand stretched
toward you and you thanked him
as if he wasn't the reason for you
nearly drowning

you still wait for him
as if he isn't the reason
your heart keeps breaking

r.h. Sin

she learned from the moon
to shine through the darkness

We Hope This Reaches You in Time

~~leave him~~
and you'll have more time
to love yourself

r.h. Sin

you were more
before you met him
so you lose nothing
when he leaves

your kind heart
took interest in someone
with cruel intentions

r.h. Sin

how many words do you hide inside silence
how many smiles do you force to hide the pain

love shouldn't feel like suffering
beneath a dark sky with no stars

r.h. Sin

You're going to fall for someone too weak to fall beside you. You're going to love someone who was never worth your emotional energy. You're going to fight for someone who would rather fight against you. You're going to find it difficult to walk away from someone who couldn't even stand beside you, but you mustn't forget that you are fully capable of standing on your own. You mustn't forget that you are capable of creating the joy that you've been searching for. You mustn't forget that it is far more important to choose yourself rather than chase after someone who will never be capable of loving you the way you deserve. Please, don't give up on yourself.

We Hope This Reaches You in Time

Real love is respecting yourself enough to move forward without the people you thought you needed. For the simple fact that they are no longer helping you find reasons to smile. You have to love yourself enough to walk away from anyone who tears you down.

r.h. Sin

Give everything you have, but never compromise your peace of mind for someone who gives you nothing.

You never realized how powerful you were until you had to learn to survive a relationship that felt more like hell. And no matter how hard it got, you continued to find ways to save yourself.

r.h. Sin

Sometimes silence is all you have. There are moments when you'll finally realize that the person you've been fighting for is no longer worthy of what you speak. There's a moment in time when you realize that they are no longer in a position to hear your thoughts and ideas. This is when your silence will then become an answer.

Real friendship is a bond with someone who cares for your peace of mind. Someone who expects nothing but is willing to give just as much as you do. Someone who simply wants you to be the best version of yourself and is committed to helping you do so. Real friendship is a bond that survives in a world where most things will end. I hope you find that. I hope that when it finally comes, when that bond finally presents itself to you, you'll be ready to accept it.

r.h. Sin

In order to live a good life, bad days must happen. In order to know happiness, you have to be familiar with sadness. There is strength in realizing what hurts you. The heartache teaches you how to let go of the things and or people who no longer serve you delight. There's a lesson in every failure. On your journey toward peace, you're going to encounter chaos, and that's fine.

Good women are tired of giving their love to people who do nothing but break their spirit. Mighty women are tired of using their strength to hold on to relationships that aren't worthy of their energy. These women are capable of walking away, and they will. These women are capable of saving themselves from those who are unworthy of their energy, and they will.

r.h. Sin

Eventually the girl you took for granted will take her love and give it to herself, and someday someone better than you will love her in all the ways you couldn't.

aren't you tired of their shit
the back and forth
not knowing where you stand
the wars, all this fighting
without the feeling of victory
all you've felt is defeat
when all you've ever wanted
was a love that keeps you
on your feet

r.h. Sin

my generation is filled
with lovers who will never know
the true meaning of love
until they find the courage
to leave behind the people
who refuse to care for their heart

relationships that feel more
like a prison term
and a happiness
that is simply a delusion
while accepting an illusion
that no longer represents
the type of relationship
that helps the soul

my generation, filled with chaos
no peace, it's difficult, it's complicated
it's nothing, it hurts, it gets worse

but you have a decision to make
and when that day comes
i hope you choose yourself

We Hope This Reaches You in Time

and so, the loneliness
will grow from the emptiness
you feel
those nights will be the toughest
those mornings, even tougher
it'll hurt, you should have loved her
but you refused to be the light
in her darkest moments

the pain you feel
will be the same heartache
you put her through
and now you know

you'll finally understand
how much it hurts
to want someone
who doesn't want you

r.h. Sin

you, reading this
your eyes dancing
on this page
you, the one who knows
how it feels
to have their heart
racing out of their chest
overrun with anxiety
desperate for relief

it is you who wants to be loved
understood for everything that you are
it is you, the one reading this
the one who is close to tears
so close to breaking

it is you who will save yourself
because this is what you've always done
because you are strong enough
to do so

he only loved you
in the dark
in secret
behind closed bedroom doors

he was yours
until he came
and then he left
whenever he was done
draining you of everything
he never deserved

aren't you tired of a love
that feels less than everything
you claimed you wanted
has your soul grown weary
of being with someone
who only wants you
for a nut
someone who comes
but never stays

your heart deserves better

r.h. Sin

sweet girl
there is a love
that will bring you peace
but sadly
this relationship
you've accepted
is not it

the broken girls
live with a story
that is hard to hear
but worthy of being heard

just listen

r.h. Sin

behind those walls
behind the barriers
that keep the world
from your heart
is a woman worth
fighting for

behind those walls
that tall, strong
separation from the world
lives a love worth
wishing for

you are greater
than what has happened
you are greater
than what occurred
in your past

behind those walls
behind that cement
that has kept others
from hurting you
like the ones from before
lives a love
that only you can provide
a love like yours
is worth climbing the wall
that sits in front
of your heart
the night will fade away

and so will the darkness
the moon will float into the abyss
and the sun will announce itself
with a ray of light and hope
and warmth and beauty

r.h. Sin

the morning will come
the day will begin
and the corners of my room
the dark corners of my room
will be filled with a light
that will kill off
all the things
and all the pain that haunts me
during the rising of the moon

the sun will sit in the sky
and it will shine
providing its light
giving me enough time
and a peace of mind
to evade you

because you live in the midnights
where i feel hopeless
filled with despair

you live in the night
the darkness, the restlessness
the air of uncertainty

We Hope This Reaches You in Time

you live in the moments
where my eyes cannot close
you survive in shattered dreams
and the bruising of my soul

but just like the night
you fade behind the horizon
and just like the sun
i rise, possibly brighter
and stronger than before

the morning will come
the day will begin
and you will be forgotten
once more

r.h. Sin

You have the right to make boundaries. You have the right to decide the lines that should never be crossed without your consent. Pay attention to those who find issues with you saying no. Pay attention to the way others react to your decision of not doing things that you don't want to do. Stay away from anyone who wants to strip you of your right to decide for yourself.

Depression is something that can dwell in places that the eyes will never be strong enough to see. Sometimes we wear masks. Smiling just to make others feel comfortable. Don't ignore what you feel. You're not weak for feeling sadness. You are not alone.

r.h. Sin

I learned that holding on to the wrong person would only prevent me from finding the right person. So many people hold on out of fear of being alone when the person they're holding on to is actually the reason for their loneliness.

I always believed that being wanted was nothing. Someone who deserves you is so much more important.

There will be men who want you, and there will be a man who truly deserves you, and it is important to know the difference.

There has never been anything wrong with feeling and or showing your sadness. It's the world around us that pressures us to smile to keep from crying. Joy has become a social construct, and laughter is often used to wall off the screams of a heart that feels pain. You don't have to hide who you are and how you feel just to make the people around you feel more comfortable. You don't have to pretend to be happy just to make yourself approachable. No matter what it is or how hard it may be. Just feel it. No more hiding.

There has never been anything wrong with feeling and or showing your sadness.

r.h. Sin

Sometimes your destiny is yourself. Sometimes the person who needs you the most is the reflection you see in the mirror. It's okay to want love, it's okay to want to be loved, but don't forget about yourself. Right now, you need you more than ever.

I used to think things got easier when the heart stopped caring, but then I realized that it actually gets better when the heart starts to care for the right people.

r.h. Sin

When a man is actually interested in a woman, she'll know because he won't leave her guessing. When a man is actually interested in a woman, there won't be any confusion. His intent will be clear, his intentions will be genuine, and there will never be a time when that woman will have to question what she means to him because he will be consistent in his effort to let her know that he cares.

just because they think
you're worthless
doesn't make it true

there are people on this earth
who will never be able
to comprehend the light in you

r.h. Sin

Stop making the wrong people feel special.
No matter how hard you try, they'll never be
right for you.

some souls
just recognize
each other

even though
they're strangers
to one another

r.h. Sin

someone will love you
in a way that everyone else
has refused to

wait for them

I think the hardest part of it all was accepting the fact that the person you cared about was never even real in the first place. People wear masks to get what they want, and once they get it, that mask falls to the floor and you're left with the struggle of letting go of someone you never actually had.

r.h. Sin

That's the problem, you like someone, you enter that relationship, then you begin to overthink and overanalyze it. Simply because that person refuses to make their own feelings clear enough to keep you from questioning their intent or the direction of that particular relationship. Don't settle for a relationship that gives you hell and keeps you up at night. Do not allow your heart to be continuously placed in hands that are uncertain about you.

Sadly, in this very moment, there is someone reading this . . . there's a woman reading this while trying to figure out why nothing works and why her effort isn't forcing some sort of change in her relationship. There's a woman dealing with this right now. Giving love to someone who chooses to hurt her. I know it's hard, but you have to remember that loving someone doesn't make them the one, and you can't expect love from someone who has chosen to take things out on you. Being torn down by your partner is not worth it. Love shouldn't feel this painful. And to be honest, if it were really love, if there were some sort of hope in your relationship, then you wouldn't even have related to everything on this page, in this book. If you're not being appreciated, it's okay to leave.

r.h. Sin

It's tough, but the reward in walking away is more peace and the opportunity to find the person who has been searching for someone like you.

Your struggles, your pain, your heartache, your frustration, your sadness. These are your truths. Your emotional truths are important. Your emotional truths do not need to be hidden, and you do not have to do this on your own.

r.h. Sin

seduce the soul and the mind first

exes are the hell you eventually leave behind

r.h. Sin

she could be soft
she could be badass
she could be both
all at once

some people are worth giving up on
it's okay to let go of the people
who no longer help you smile

r.h. Sin

love should feel like
a midnight showing
at the cinema

We Hope This Reaches You in Time

I think I laughed then cried. There was both good and bad, but not enough good to make me want to stay with you.

r.h. Sin

It took me years to realize that all the people who were trying to tear me down were always below me, and I hadn't noticed this until I heard their voices beneath my feet.

you see him
not as he really is
but who you want him to be
and this is why you stay
longer than you should

hoping for a change
that can't happen
holding on, claiming to be in love
when all you ever feel is pain

r.h. Sin

it got harder to stay
the moment i began
to love me
more than you could

The only time you should give up on the person you love is if that person refuses to care for you properly. So many people are hurting for a love that doesn't even feel like love in the first place.

r.h. Sin

Don't let a bad individual stop you from being a good person.

Don't let a bad relationship keep you from finding your soul mate.

Don't let a bad experience with someone who belongs to your past ruin your future.

i tried
i fought
i loved
i forgave
i stayed
nothing changed
i'm tired

r.h. Sin

Some people enter your life, only to show you
what happens when you settle for less than you
deserve.

Loving someone who hurts you is not ideal. There's nothing beautiful about falling for someone too weak to catch you. There's nothing intriguing about a so-called love that damages your heart.

r.h. Sin

She caught fire then torched her demons.

She led lions and wolves. She had the courage to rip through fear.

r.h. Sin

Any man who says he's not looking for a relationship but expects you to treat him like your boyfriend is overrated, underwhelming, and never worth it.

she's powerful
she's just tired
of breaking down

r.h. Sin

You're afraid of being alone, and so you've found yourself falling for someone who never intended to catch you. What hurts the most is that you've done just about all that you can and yet your every effort is met with disappointment and heartache. Your heart has stretched itself to its limit, and your soul is trying to cope with this feeling . . . of feeling nothing. You've been fighting for a love that isn't love. You've been fighting for a love that makes you hate yourself. You've been sitting on the edge of breaking down while struggling to hold yourself together. I hope these words reach you in time. I hope you read this knowing that these words were written especially for you, because if you're looking for a sign, this is it. A reminder that you are fully capable of walking away from anyone who refuses to stand by your side. You deserve better than the relationship you've settled for.

Evolving and growing as an individual will cost you unhealthy relationships and toxic friendships. People will say you changed just to make you feel bad for being greater than they expected you to be, but that's entirely okay. You have to learn to be happy with who you are becoming even when others want you to remain the same.

r.h. Sin

I was in love with the echo of everything you used to pretend to be.

It took years of being without you to finally understand that the best moments of my life were yet to come. In your absence, I would eventually rediscover my own peace and what it took to finally fall for someone strong enough to fall beside me.

Then it dawned on me. I never knew love while being with you. I never knew love while entertaining the relationships that were never really worthy of my time or dedication. It was never love, it wasn't real. It was something I accepted. It was the illusion that I believed in because I was afraid of being alone, but then I realized that the most painful part of loneliness was being with someone who was never actually mine to begin with.

There are many surprises in life, some of which we can't see because holding on to the wrong person blocks our view of something better. I know it's not easy, I know it's extremely difficult to sometimes see a life without the person you thought you needed, but walking away is necessary. Walking away will bring you closer to yourself and closer to the relationship you've always wanted.

I know this for a fact because I would have never met my wife if I hadn't let go of toxic and unhealthy relationships. We would have not met each other if it wasn't for our ability to finally move on and let go.

I hope you find a truth in this book that helps you build enough courage to walk away. I hope you find some sort of advice or mantra to live by within these pages.

This is not the end . . . this is actually the beginning . . . .

r.h. Sin

We Hope This Reaches You in Time

Andrews McMeel Publishing
a division of Andrews McMeel Universal
1130 Walnut Street, Kansas City, Missouri 64106

www.andrewsmcmeel.com

20 21 22 23 24 RR2 10 9 8 7 6 5 4 3 2 1

ISBN: 978-1-5248-5576-5

Library of Congress Control Number: 2019948372

Editor: Patty Rice
Art Director: Diane Marsh
Production Editor: Elizabeth A. Garcia
Production Manager: Cliff Koehler